Irrational Behavioral Economics

Predicting the Unpredictable

By Naven Johnson

Copyright © 2018 by Naven Johnson

All rights reserved. This book or any portion thereof may not be reproduced or used in any manner whatsoever without the express written permission of the publisher except for the use of brief quotations in a book review.

Printed in the United States of America

First Printing, 2018

Table of Contents

Part 1 4
Part 2 7
Part 3 11
Part 4 14
Part 5 27
Part 6 34
Conclusion 39

Part 1

Importance of Behavioral Economics

Do we always make rational choices? In other words: are all human's homo economicus? Certainly not. But this was not so obvious until the beginning of XX century, when the behavioral economics was developed. Behavioral Economics is a group of concepts which put into question the rational character of people's financial decisions.

Nowadays, behavioral economics concepts are used in many various fields:

Personal and public finances. "Save more tomorrow" is a program aiming at increasing pension savings among employees, by visualizing a future situation to the people. It is based on the Behavioral Economics findings: firstly, showing the reason of the situation: that people are too optimistic about their future (so therefore they save too little) and secondly by providing a tool to solve the problem: when confronted with a vision of the future people start being more realistic about their future.

Health. Campaigns towards giving up alcohol drinking are often based on Behavioral Economics concepts. For example, when an advertisement uses statistics comparing the amount of alcohol drank in different countries this changes the alcohol overuse issue from an individual to a common, society wide problem. In this situation, the following Behavioral Economics assumption was applied: social norms signal appropriate behavior in a situation of a whole community in danger.

Energy. Climate change: it is hard for people to perceive the long-term consequences of their actions, especially when the feedback to their everyday actions towards the goal is not visible. Feedback is needed. Based on this knowledge a solution was easy to find: a carbon footprint calculator was developed, showing how many trees you need to plant in order to absorb carbon dioxide emissions produced, day by day, action by action.

Marketing. Many examples can be provided. The most Behavioral Economics applications are within marketing and this is what this book puts its main attention to. A marketing campaign of any product can become more effective when it deploys scientifically proven concepts. However, before we move to the very examples, we need to acquaint ourselves with a theoretical background of Behavioral Economics in order to better understand the importance of Behavioral Economics in the field of marketing.

Part 2

Grounding Assumptions of Behavioral Economics

The human decision making process is full of biases as a result of the way people think and feel. Behavioral Economics stays in a contrary to the homo economicus concept created by economists. This is one of the most basic economic concepts. It assumes that a human makes rational decisions, i.e. his choices are a result of the rational decisions such as price, alternative cost and benefit. Rational choice takes place by combining cost minimization together with benefit maximization.

However, nowadays numerous transactions take place online. We have access to an enormous set of data. We can analyze the decision-making process of a customer, divided into tiny parts, taking into account even so called "micro moments". This data shows clearly, that the majority of our purchases are spontaneous and far away from being a rational, deeply thought over decision. This is what Behavioral Economics focuses on: the biases as a result of the way people think and feel. According to Behavioral Economics the optimal decisions, where the person choses maximum benefit at the minimum cost rarely exists. Generally speaking, people tend to make decisions by sufficing and satisfying (satisficing) rather than optimizing. The selfish, rational economic choice is affected and disturbed by emotional factors and the social dimension.

We make economic decisions based for instance on:
what other people think about the product (based on clients' opinions and recommendations),
what we think other people would think about us if we bought the product,
what we like about the product at the very first sight; it is often non-rational.

This was just an example of why people make purchase decisions not directly referring to the product value itself. However, the number of ways our rational decision is affected by non-rational factors explains reasons why the homo economicus concept is very often inapplicable. Remember, the human decision making process is full of biases as a result of the way people think and feel.

We are poor predictors of future behavior.
We are social animals; trust, fairness, norms, self-consistency and commitment is very important to us; often more important than the simple cost-benefit comparison of an economic decision.
We have insufficient knowledge.

We have limited resources of time and therefore we tend to use mental shortcuts - we make decisions choosing only one aspect and ignoring others.
We are feedback addicted.
Our brain's' processing capacity is limited.

Our own connotations to the product and the way it is advertised are based on our cultural background, preferences and experiences.

Readily available information in our memory is the simplest way to make a decision. Not the most rational but the simplest and quickest and therefore we take it.

Context of a situation in which we make a decision strongly influences the way we perceive costs and benefits or relational truth about the circumstances.

We have problems with understanding big amounts: we better understand one loss than 1000 loses. 1000 is irrational to our brain and therefore less important than one. The reason is our thinking pattern which evolved from our early ancestors living in small groups.

Biases can be also divided into the following categories: decision making, belief and behavioral biases, social biases and memory biases - impaired recall of a memory.

Part 3

History of Behavioral Economics development

The first works on psychological aspects of economic decisions were conducted long before the Nobel Memory Prize winners started their work on Perception Theory in the 1970s. It was already of economists' interest in the XVIIIth-XIXth century. However, the neoclassical revolution of economics at the beginning of the XXth century diminished interest on the psychology and economics interconnections for a long time, turning it onto the economic connections with nature sciences.

Again, an increased interest in connections between psychology and economics arose in the 1950s. Herbert Simon developed a bounded rationality concept, claiming that the decision process of every human is environment-driven. Gerd Gigerenzer further developed the concept by researching effects of this fact. He claimed, that the way our early ancestors functioned still influence our decision-making process - they needed to make quick decisions in order to survive in the unhostile world.

Behavioral Economics development was importantly accelerated with the revolutionary discoveries within neuroscience. It unveiled the mystery of how the decision-making process is made by our brain, showing, that during the process brain parts responsible for emotional thinking are very active. This discovery provided the necessary proof to the behavioral economics theories - it was shown that human brain is no longer the rational thinking shelter.

Neuroscience discovered how the decision-making process is made by our brain - what is typical to any human in the world. This is bounded rationality created unconsciously by our brains, affected by the thousands of years of evolution and experience gathered by our ancestors throughout this time; adaptation of humans to the changing environment shaped an important subconscious decision making factor.

Looking back, we can see that Tversky and Kahneman had a strong basis for the development of the nowadays behavioral economics. However, their role was inevitable: the strong methodological frames provided by a huge number of empirical experiments conducted by those researchers is what made the behavioral economics a commonly accepted concept. Their discoveries became appreciated with the highest prize in science: the Nobel Prize. Key assumptions of the winning theory: (1) Human willingness to take risk is influenced by the way in which choices are framed - it is context dependent. (2) Gain framing vs loss framing; default framing vs your own assessment of situation framing.

Part 4

Main theoretical concepts within Behavioral Economics

Within Behavioral Economics one can extract the three main areas of interest: heuristics, framing and the market inefficiencies. Shortly saying:

- The heuristics concept focuses on the pattern of functioning of the so called mental shortcuts very often used by people in need of an instant decision. This is actually a big part of people's decisions.
- Framing concept focuses on the cultural contextualization, so called social filter of a decision-making process.
- Market inefficiencies focus on the biases associated to the market functioning.

Heuristics

Heuristics are mental shortcuts, focusing on chosen aspects of approximate calculation - both conscious and unconscious. A broader definition of heuristics explains the way humans deal with incomplete information and time constraints - they focus on a chosen aspect of a problem to make a decision. It's obvious that in everyday life people don't have the time and resources to investigate all aspects or reach all the necessary data points. Therefore, we need to rely on our thoughts, assumptions and beliefs. Based on our experiences and knowledge about the environment we live in we often guess right. Heuristics are simply a must to survive.

There are two types of situations where heuristics are used:
Instant, spontaneous decisions - when the person is not aware of the cognitive bias going on,
Well-thought decisions; a person is aware of the limited knowledge, time or financial resources and therefore

consciously make a decision based on his beliefs and intuitive or subjective judgments

Heuristics can be understood in the following dimensions: cognitive dimensions, emotional dimensions, social dimensions, homo-economicus dimensions. Unconscious, instant decisions are made based on the first three dimensions. The whole rational thinking process takes place based on all four dimensions.

Important theories developed based on the Heuristics concept:

Theory of information processing (Behavioral Economics) developed in 1970s by Amos Tversky and Daniel Kahneman was in contrary to the traditional economics theory of homo economicus with rational choices. A paper named "Judgment Under Uncertainty: Heuristics and Biases", describing this concept was published in 1974. It laid the ground for a sharp development of Behavioral Economics. The Nobel Memory Prize was awarded in 2002 for the development of a Prospect Theory. It pointed out three heuristics: available information, cognitive limitations and time constraints.

Prospect Theory - explains the importance of the alternative choices for framing the results of a decision-making process. A Nobel Prize was awarded to Kahneman and Tversky for the development of this theory in 2002.

Dual-system theory - this theory explains the way that non-rational decisions are made. It divides the thinking process into two (separate and significantly different from each other) parts. The first one is the so-called system one thinking process. This part of the decision-making process is the so called "default process". It is instant, implicit, unconscious, associative, contextual, domain specific, independent of working memory, non-logical and parallel. It has a large capacity; low effort is needed to conduct this part.

The second part of the decision making process comes always after the first one. It is impossible for humans to eliminate the first part of the process and more importantly it is often that the whole decision making process is finalized with the end of the first part - system one. The second part is where we start being rational, i.e. we take into account benefits and costs and compare them consciously. This part of the process takes place where an instant decision is not needed. The main characteristics of system two thinking is a total contrary to the system one thinking part: it involves conscious reasoning, weighing of options, and comparisons. It is controlled, slow, inhibitory, rule-based, abstract, domain general, linked to language, logical and serial. It involves high effort, but has a small capacity and is limited by working memory capacity.

Dual-system theory specifies the following biases appearing during the whole decision making process:
Availability (internal bias factor) system 1
Affect (internal bias factor) system 1
Salience (external bias factor) system 1

Status quo and inertia: humans' desire to keep the status quo

Availability - It is the most profound reason why our brain make this and not other decisions. Our ancestors needed to make quick decisions in order to survive, living a harsh hunters life. Only information available within the instant memory could be sufficient to make a decision: stay and fight or escape. This bias is happening within the system one thinking process.

Affect - This bias is connected with our emotions. This is an automatic word-judgment relation. happening within the system one thinking process. Sometimes this association is so powerful, that the system two thinking process is not even allowed to start by our brain when it is focused on an emotion. Humans are certainly not emotion rulers.

Salience - Importance of information provided. It is an external bias factor happening within the system one thinking process.

Status quo. People are unwilling to change things as they are. They chose what they know. Why? Explanation is simple: automatic behavioral patterns are a result of repetition and associative learning. This is how habits are formed. It is the unconscious rationalization of a decision. The inertia concept provides an answer why people tend to stay at status quo. People are inertia dependent. They prefer to not make an active choice, as it can harm their safety, their status quo. This is why the default options are so popular. It is happening within the system one thinking process.

"Bounded rationality": Deviations from: logic, probability and rational choice theory leading to so called "cognitive biases". Cognitive limitations (Herbert A. Simon).

Mental accounting - relative to many factors around the decision-making process; not only object-based. Taking care of not only the very product offered, but of the value of the whole transaction process may increase the interest in a product. The compared costs and benefits associated with the product can change in a positive or negative way depending on the transaction process quality.

"Irrational" Decision Making - The irrational decision making concept describes the irrational consumer behavior in reference to price vs value perception. Many proofs of the concept can be found in a book by Dan Ariely called "Predictably Irrational".

Framing

Framing claims that an individual perception is affected by the social and cultural "filter" or the environment person grew up in. This can be influenced by influences such as mass media, politics, and cultural background. It is a social construction of the world created by a society and the individual.

There can be two types of framing: frames in thought (simplification of reality) and frames in communication (packaging facts with a specific person's view of the world). When several people with a distinct framing come together we come closer to the objective truth, as different interpretations of the same facts are made, cultural and societal framing collapses. Frames in communication - subjective interpretation of objective facts is necessary to make the information understandable and of any use to the audience.

Market inefficiencies

An efficient market hypothesis says that the price fully reflects the available information. Loss aversion, overconfidence, overreaction. According to behavioral economists a market is subject to numerous biases, which can be divided into three main blocks: structural factors, behavioral biases and calendar effects. Structural factors are the fundamental ones such as unfair competition, lack of market transparency, regulatory actions, etc. Behavioral biases of the market factors such as too optimistic forecasting or adopting personal and social norms to the market decisions. Calendar effects are these which can be spotted in stock returns from year to year or month to month, such as the January effect.

Market inefficiencies are the non-rational economic/purchase decisions. Market inefficiencies concept puts into question the efficient-market hypothesis.

Concepts of Behavioral Economics within the market inefficiencies area:

Limited Knowledge and importance of feedback. Feedback importance: research results have shown that people have problems with perceiving long term consequences of their actions. People don't quit smoking despite the informational campaigns on its harmful consequences. Based on this knowledge, a solution was easy to find: stop smoking smartphone applications helped to show the day by day (short-term) health benefits from giving up smoking, such as gradually diminishing threat of serious diseases.

Psychology of Price. Our decisions are strongly conditioned and influenced by the way in which choices are presented. Predictably Irrational and Nudge, elaborated by the Nobel Prize Winners, Kahneman and Tversky, are important sources of information on this concept.

Temporal Dimensions (forecasting and memory; time discounting; present bias; hot-cold empathy gap). Forecasting - humans are not good at predicting future events, as we do not learn easily from our experience. We are always too optimistic about the future. A very good example is how we tend to underestimate time needed to complete tasks, despite experiencing the underestimation problem many times before. Explanation: our memory tends to keep only the good things and clean up the bad things (as the failure of wrong estimation of time needed to complete a task). Present bias - our future self is more responsible than our present self. I can start a diet tomorrow, I can start exercising next month, I can start saving money in two months. Everyone made such promises and was 100% sure that they are going to achieve the goal, but end up failing. Explanation: we tend to devalue the future benefits and are good at assessing present costs. Therefore, the cost of going to a gym today is assessed correctly, but the benefit is underestimated. As a result, the cost-benefit relation in our perception is far more negative than it is in reality.

Social dimensions (trust and dishonesty; fairness and reciprocity; social norms; consistency). People are strongly affected by the reciprocity effect. They tend to be fair, as they expect the same from the other side. And such relations help to meet one of the most basic needs of a human being - safety.

A recently developed adaptive market theory tries to explain the behavioral distortions within the traditional efficient-market hypothesis as actually rational. Lo, the founder of the adaptive market theory claims that many from the so called behavioral biases of the market factors are actually not biases but rational reaction (adaptation) to the quickly changing environment.

Part 5

Application of Behavioral Economics Concepts in Marketing - real life examples

We got to the core of this article - having the theoretical background of Behavioral Economics we can think about the possible applications of Behavioral Economics in marketing. The examples are divided by the most basic marketing strategy elements: product, price, place (distribution), and promotion.

PRODUCT - Description of a product, graphic presentation of a product

Mental Accounting: Paying with a card instead of with cash - decoupling the purchase process from payment. The compared costs and benefits are not only perceived in relation to the product, but also to the whole purchase process. Cost is perceived as much smaller as we do not pay in cash. Therefore, the limit value of the benefit required to attract the client can be smaller while paying with a card compared to paying with cash.

Memory: It was found that changes in experiences happened only to induce happiness temporarily as we got used to the new situation. Advertisers use this Behavioral Economics discovery: for instance, they change their product's packaging from time to time. They know that even a slightly new version of a product can draw back attention.

Inertia and Status Quo: When installing a new program a majority will go for the default version. More functions will be installed if we need to uncheck the unwanted functions than if we need to check the desired functions. In general, people tend to choose the default version. The explanation to this situation lies in the Inertia concept - unwillingness to make decisions, as it implies taking risk. It is safer to choose the recommended option, and safety is the most basic human need.

PRICE - price of a product

"Irrational" Decision Making: The power of a free product; when something costed $10 and now costs $1 compared to being reduced from $0.99 to 0$, The majority of customers will choose the free product. Even though the cost difference is very similar and $1 is a cost which is not even noticeable.

PLACE (DISTRIBUTION) - the whole transaction process quality

Mental Accounting - taking care of not only the very product offered, but of the value of the whole transaction process may increase the interest in a product. The compared costs and benefits associated with the product change in a positive or negative way - depending on the transaction process quality. Think about being served by an unqualified, rude seller.

Hot-cold empathy gap. When a customer is in a hot state of mind, he is unable to make a reasonable decision, due to emotions. Marketers try to put the client into this state of mind, by stimulating the senses, for example by playing music or introducing a scent of flowers. Ethics of such marketing activity is another issue.

Identity economics. People have a strong need of a continuous and consistent self-image. Therefore, when humans fail to keep it, they try their best to rationalize their decisions and cheat their mind. This concept is known in Behavioral Economics as a process called cognitive dissonance reduction.

PROMOTION - all the activities which goal is to advertise the product

Dual system theory: the concept of an external bias factor, salience of information. It can be widely used in marketing. For example, a properly designed brand name may infer quality - it can create mental shortcuts to the receiver of information. Potential clients have a positive association with the company's name even before they learn about the product and this undoubtedly increases the probability of a purchase.

Another example shows also the salience bias, but this time we focus on its visual aspect. When a lower price is written in a smaller font than the regular price it can increase the perception of the discounted price.

Feedback importance. Humans like to see the potential effect of the action before making a decision. We need to have a feedback or see results. An example of advertisement and applying it: firstly, showing a person with a headache, then a person taking the advertised painkiller and finalizing the add with a visualization of a happy, pain-free person, who took the pill. This is how advertisements very often apply Behavioral Economics: they use the pattern of showing the pre and post-purchase situations of a person.

Present Bias. Behavioral Economics research results show that present events are weighted more heavily than future ones, as the future is blurry and very much intangible. People prefer getting smaller but quicker over bigger but later benefits. Marketers should offer instant rewards. It is less important how big the reward is and much more important how quickly it can be obtained.

Social Factor. Fairness and reciprocity. Giving something for free (e.q. an Ebook or tutorial) makes the customer more willing to buy. It is exactly due to fairness and reciprocity patterns subconsciously followed by humans - somebody gives me something then I need to be fair and give him something in return. People have so called inequity aversion. This is why giving free stuff to people is so important when it comes to selling products.

Identity economics. Behavioral Economics proved that humans prefer to create a consistent self-image, as this is what social norms rewards. In advertisements, we can many times see examples of satisfied customers. The more similar he is to the target group customers, the better effect of an advertisement.

Part 6

Next goal of Behavioral Economics - application for public policies

Starting from the 90s behavioral economics has become a subject to a sharply increasing interest. Many scientists, both economists and psychologists started conduct of empirical researches within the field of behavioral economics.

One of them is Nava Ashraf, Assistance Professor at the London School of Economics. While working in Africa, she met a women, who had problems with saving money and came up with a simple solution: she gave the key for her savings box to her neighbor; each time she was tempted to withdraw some money she had this second person acting as her savings-guard. This simple example of how the "inter-temporal choice" was fought, inspired Nava Ashraf to use the idea on a much larger scale.

She worked together with a Philippines-based bank to change saving patterns of their clients. The bank developed a campaign where it encouraged people to save money by providing the opportunity of an "inter-temporal choice". Clients were offered a save box, where they could determine the date of withdrawal, but could not change it. This campaign gave great results, allowing many people to finally meet their savings goals. Why was the campaign a success? It was based on a present bias concept. Our future self is more responsible than our present self – we can use this knowledge to prevent us from making a mistake.

Not only does the scientific world use behavioral economics to deal with real-life, society-wide problems. As behavioral economics gets more recognition, its concepts reach various groups. Among them are civil servants, who start noticing the potential of using psychological knowledge in the process of designing public policies. One of them is Lawrence Summers. While working as a U.S. Treasury Secretary, he changed an opt-in form to an opt-out version, making the opt-out alternative a default one. As a result, the share of companies using the program increased, following the pattern explained by the dual-system theory.

Lawrence Summers understood the importance of thinking small. He made use of the psychological, "irrational" aspects of the decision-making process. Summers actions gave good results and they were achieved only thanks to his knowledge about behavioral economics concepts, in his examples which were derived from evolutionary psychology. Behavioral economics power comes from the interdisciplinarity of its concepts.

Examples presented by Nava Ashraf and Lawrence Summers clearly show that behavioral economics can be of a great assistance, not only to explain a single person's behavior, but it can be also extended to understand and influence people to move in the desired direction when there are large groups. However, turning to behavioral economics is tough. As Sendhil Mullainathan, professor of economics at the Harvard University, explains: Economists and others who engage in policy debates like to wrangle about big issues on the macroscopic level. Why is it this way? The answer is simple. It requires a revolutionary change of mindset to allow framing to be treated as important as the well-thought, long-developed policy.

Economists and politicians have a difficult time understanding that the graphics following a new law proposal can be decisive for support of the idea or its lack thereof. Let us take as an example a bank, who decided to perform a contextual research before establishing a new rate on loans. The bank had send thousands of letters to their clients. Randomly selecting groups of clients who received new loan proposals significantly differing by the loan rate level. The difference in the loan rate level was followed by a different graphic design of the letter. For instance, some of the letters had a photo of a woman, some of a man. Results of the actions were stunning, clearly showing the impact of the proposal framing on the decision made by clients. As Mullainathan says: A woman's photo instead of a man's increased demand among men by as much as dropping the interest rate five points!

Conclusion

Homo economicus is dead, killed by Behavioral Economics discoveries. And so, the Smith's invisible hand of a market is put into question.

Behavioral economics suggests a change of the mindset of civil servants and politics towards the economic policies: from the policies based on the Smith's invisible hand of the market to a more regulative approach. Thousands of examples of empirical research show that the Vilfred Pareto 's classical welfare theorem does not hold truth in the real world. The invisible hand of the market simply does not ensure maximization. The price of a product is not an optimal point being a result of rational decisions made by the seller and the client.

Behavioral Economics proves, that market doesn't really endeavor to maximize the total welfare, but, very often, to the maximization of seller's revenue, at the cost of the client. Why is that? The answer lies in information asymmetry. Sellers possess the knowledge about clients' psychology and know how to use it. They mastered the marketing actions, being able to direct the client in the desired direction. As the advertisements become more and more sophisticated, people buy more than they need, at a higher price than they should and often end up buying stuff they do not even need, driven by the moment.

Actors on the market are not at all rational in their choices. But there is a solution to this problem - politicians should acknowledge the problem coming with the information asymmetry and act against it. Firstly, there is a strong need for a more regulatory approach and secondly for informational campaigns, balancing the information asymmetry. In both situations, behavioral economics can be of much assistance. It can be applied by public institutions to produce and implement necessary regulations.

Homo economicus is dead. This statement is true, but we should be aware, that it does not apply to the entire world population. Social norms differ from region to region. For instance, the very profound difference is the degree to which humans make rational choices on the market. It was found, that people living in the western world are much more homo economicus that the people from South-East Asia. The majority of Behavioral Economics research has been conducted in the USA and Europe, therefore marketing strategies based on Behavioral Economics assumptions may not work in other parts of the world. Behavioral Economics is a relatively young field of science and therefore much more research is needed in order to simply transfer its successful solutions between the countries.

Generalization of Behavioral Economics findings is thus impossible to apply in all the geographical regions. But the remedy to this problem is coming. The advanced analytical tools are available and the enormous amount of data, the big data world, is at the fingertips thanks to the widespread of the internet. Taking an example of marketing, each company can develop its own marketing strategy, based on the behavioral and transactional information derived from the visitor's' action on the website or customer's reaction to an email campaign. Checking the subpages with the highest click through rate? Checking the specific links clicked within an email? Nowadays it is not a problem and the analytical tools available make it possible to simply, at low cost, and most importantly, instantly, provide us with a set of useful statistics and what is more it is even able to automatically arrange marketing actions according to the customer's behavioral and transactional profile. Behavioral Economics applications have never been easier.

www.ingramcontent.com/pod-product-compliance
Lightning Source LLC
Chambersburg PA
CBHW030038230526
45472CB00002B/575